Police Officers

By Jacqueline Laks Gorman

Reading consultant: Susan Nations, M.Ed., author/literacy coach/consultant

Gareth Stevens
Publishing

Please visit our Web site www.garethstevens.com. For a free color catalog of all our high-quality books, call toll free 1-800-542-2595 or fax 1-877-542-2596.

Library of Congress Cataloging-in-Publication Data

Gorman, Jacqueline Laks, 1955-
    Police officer / by Jacqueline Laks Gorman.
        p. cm. — (People in my community)
    Summary: Explains what police officers do, including helping people
in trouble, stopping people who break the law, and directing traffic.
    Includes bibliographical references and index.
    ISBN: 978-1-4339-3351-6 (pbk.)
    ISBN: 978-1-4339-3352-3 (6-pack)
    ISBN: 978-1-4339-3350-9 (library binding)
    1. Police—Juvenile literature. [1. Police.   2. Occupations.]   I. Title.
    HV7922.G67   2002
    363.2'2—dc21   2002024622

New edition published 2010 by
Gareth Stevens Publishing
111 East 14th Street, Suite 349
New York, NY 10003

New text and images this edition copyright © 2010 Gareth Stevens Publishing

Original edition published 2003 by Weekly Reader® Books
An imprint of Gareth Stevens Publishing
Original edition text and images copyright © 2003 Gareth Stevens Publishing

Art direction: Haley Harasymiw, Tammy Gruenewald
Page layout: Michael Flynn, Katherine A. Goedheer
Editorial direction: Kerri O'Donnell, Diane Laska Swanke

Photo credits: Cover, back cover, p. 1 © Darrin Klimek/Digital Vision/Getty Images; pp. 5, 15 ©
Shutterstock.com; pp. 7, 9, 11, 13, 17, 19, 21 by Gregg Andersen.

Printed in the United States of America

CPSIA compliance information: Batch #CR217260GS: For further information contact Gareth Stevens, New York, New York at 1-800-542-2595.

Table of Contents

An Important Job 4

Police Gear 8

A Safe Neighborhood 10

Glossary 22

For More Information 23

Index 24

Boldface words appear in the glossary.

An Important Job

A police officer has an important job. A police officer helps people.

A police officer helps people in trouble. A police officer helps keep people safe.

Police Gear

Police officers wear **badges** and special **uniforms**. They use radios to talk to each other.

radio

A Safe Neighborhood

Police officers stop people who break the **law**. They help keep your **neighborhood** safe.

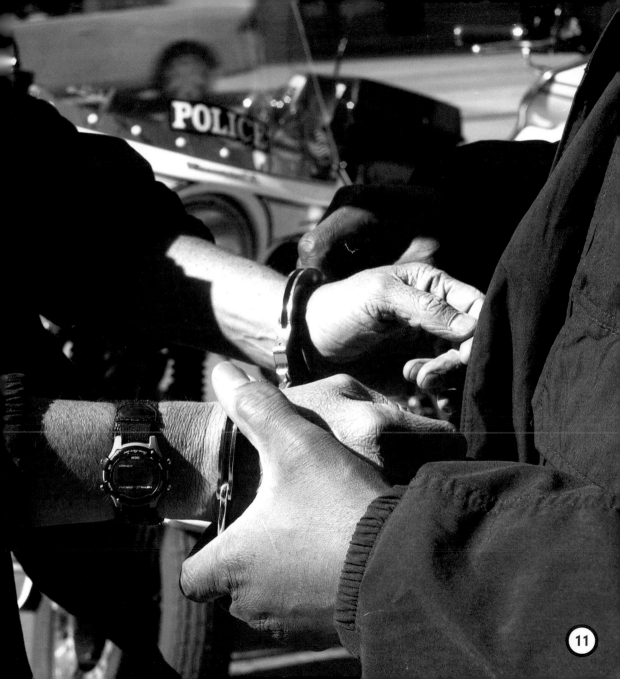

Some police officers ride in police cars. Some ride on motorcycles.

motorcycles

Sometimes police officers direct traffic. They give tickets to drivers who drive too fast.

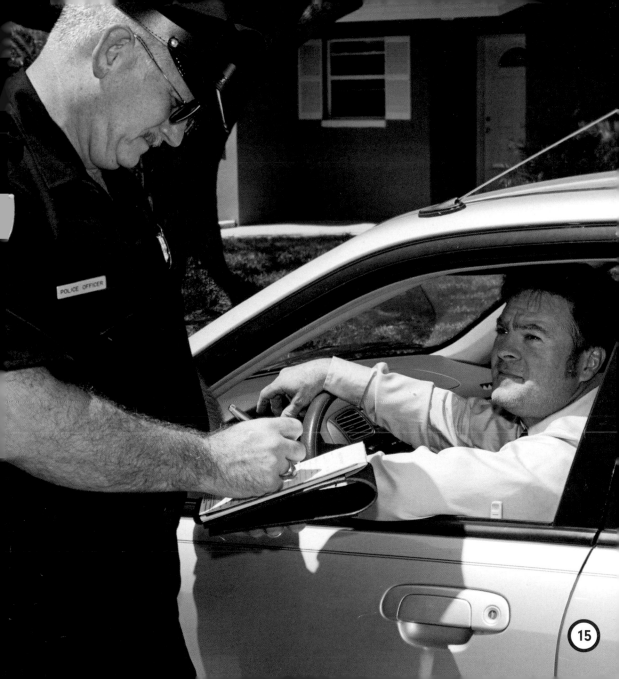

Sometimes police officers visit schools. They talk about how to stay safe.

If you are ever lost or need help, a police officer can help you.

Would you like to be a police officer?

Glossary

badge: a small sign that identifies people and is pinned to their clothes

law: a rule that people follow

neighborhood: the streets and homes around the place you live

uniform: clothing worn by members of a group such as firefighters, mail carriers, or police officers

For More Information

Books

Bourgeois, Paulette. *Police Officers.*
    Toronto, ON: Kids Can Press, 2004.
Braithwaite, Jill. *Police Cars.*
    Minneapolis, MN: Lerner Publications, 2004.
Gorman, Jacqueline Laks. *Why Do We Have Laws?*
    New York: Gareth Stevens Publishing, 2008.
McMahon, Kara. *Police Officers!*
    New York: Random House, 2006.

Web Sites

Free Police and Safety Coloring and Activity Pages
http://kids.askacop.org/coloringpages.html

Index

law 10
motorcycles 12, 13
neighborhood 10
police cars 12
radios 8, 9
tickets 14

traffic 14
uniforms 8
visits from police
   officers 16
work of police officers
   4, 6, 10, 14, 16

About the Author

Jacqueline Laks Gorman is a writer and editor. She grew up in New York City and began her career working on encyclopedias and other reference books. Since then, she has worked on many different kinds of books. She lives with her husband and children, Colin and Caitlin, in DeKalb, Illinois.